INTRODUCTION

Butterflies and moths belong to the second largest order of insects (next to beetles) with approximately 170,000 species worldwide. All have two pairs of wings covered with overlapping layers of fine scales. They feed by uncoiling a long feeding tube (proboscis) and sucking nutrients from flowers, puddles, etc. When not in use, the tube is coiled under the head.

The two groups differ in several ways:

BUTTERFLIES
- Active by day
- Brightly colored
- Thin body
- Rests with wings held erect over its back
- Antennae are thin and thickened at the tip

MOTHS
- Active at night
- Most are dull-colored
- Stout body
- Rests with wings folded, tent-like, over its back
- Antennae are usually thicker and often feathery

All butterflies and moths have a complex life cycle consisting of four developmental stages.

1. **EGGS** – Eggs are laid singly or in clusters on vegetation or on the ground. One or more clutches of eggs may be laid each year.
2. **CATERPILLARS (LARVAE)** – These worm-like creatures hatch from eggs and feed primarily on plants (often on the host plant on which the eggs were laid). As they grow, larvae shed their skin periodically.
3. **PUPAE** – Pupae are the "cases" within which caterpillars transform into adults. The pupa of a butterfly is known as a chrysalis; those of moths are called cocoons. In cooler regions, pupae often overwinter before maturing into butterflies or moths.
4. **ADULT** – Butterflies/moths emerge from pupae to feed and breed.

ATTRACTING BUTTERFLIES TO YOUR YARD

1. **Food** – Almost all butterfly caterpillars eat plants; adult butterflies feed almost exclusively on plant nectar. Your local garden shop, library and bookstore will have information on which plants attract specific species.
2. **Water** – Soak the soil in your garden or sandy areas to create puddles. These provide a source of water and minerals.
3. **Rocks** – Put large flat rocks in sunny areas. Butterflies will gather there to spread their wings and warm up.
4. **Brush** – Small brush piles and hollow logs provide ideal places for butterflies to lay their eggs and hibernate over the winter.

Waterford Press produces reference guides that introduce novices to nature, science, outdoor recreation and survival. Product information is featured on the website: **www.waterfordpress.com**.

Text and illustrations © 2020 by Waterford Press Inc. All rights reserved. Cover image © Shutterstock.
To order, call 800-434-2555.
For permissions, or to share comments, e-mail editor@waterfordpress.com. For information on custom-published products, call 800-434-2555 or e-mail info@waterfordpress.com.

A POCKET NATURALIST® GUIDE

MASSACHUSETTS BUTTERFLIES & POLLINATORS

MASSACHUSETTS BUTTERFLIES & POLLINATORS

Kavanagh/Leung

A Folding Pocket Guide to Familiar Species

T0123977

SWALLOWTAILS & ALLIES

This family includes the largest butterfly species. Most are colorful and have a tail-like projection on each hindwing.

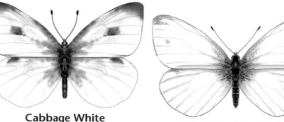

Pipevine Swallowtail
Battus philenor
To 3.5 in. (9 cm)
Note white crescent-shaped marks on outer edge of hindwings.

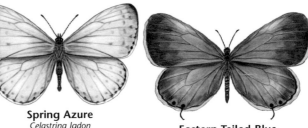

Black Swallowtail
Papilio polyxenes
To 3.5 in. (9 cm)
Note two rows of yellow spots on forewings and orange spots on hindwings.

Eastern Tiger Swallowtail
Papilio glaucus
To 6 in. (15 cm)

Spicebush Swallowtail
Papilio troilus
To 4.5 in. (11 cm)
Note greenish hindwings.

Zebra Swallowtail
Eurytides marcellus
To 3.5 in. (9 cm)
Note white-tipped "tails" and red spot near base of hindwings.

Giant Swallowtail
Papilio cresphontes
To 6 in. (15 cm)
One of the largest North American butterflies.

WHITES & SULPHURS

White and yellow/orange butterflies are among the first to appear in spring.

Falcate Orangetip
Anthocharis midea
To 1.5 in. (4 cm)

Veined White
Artogeia napi
To 1.5 in. (4 cm)

WHITES & SULPHURS

Cabbage White
Pieris rapae
To 2 in. (5 cm)
One of the most common butterflies.

West Virginia White
Pieris virginiensis
To 2.25 in. (5.2 cm)
Springtime butterfly inhabits moist woodlands.

Mustard White
Artogeia oleracea
To 2 in. (5 cm)
Common in moist forests. Feeds on a variety of mustards.

Cloudless Sulphur
Phoebis sennae
To 3 in. (8 cm)
Common in open areas and fields.

Clouded Sulphur
Colias philodice
To 2 in. (5 cm)
Common in open areas and along roadsides.

Orange Sulphur
Colias eurytheme
To 2.5 in. (6 cm)
Gold-orange butterfly has a prominent forewing spot.

Little Yellow
Eurema lisa
To 1.5 in. (4 cm)

Pink-Edged Sulphur
Colias interior
To 1.75 in. (4.2 cm)

GOSSAMER-WINGED BUTTERFLIES

This family of small bluish or coppery butterflies often has small, hair-like tails on its hindwings. Most rest with their wings folded and underwings exposed.

Spring Azure
Celastrina ladon
To 1.3 in. (3.6 cm)
One of the earliest spring butterflies.

Eastern Tailed Blue
Cupido comyntas
To 1 in. (3 cm)
Note orange spots above thread-like hindwing tails.

Silvery Blue
Glaucopsyche lygdamus
To 1.25 in. (3.2 cm)
Upperwings are blue with a black maginal band.
Underwings

American Copper
Lycaena phlaeas
To 1.25 in. (3.2 cm)
Common in disturbed areas and along roadsides.

Brown Elfin
Incisalia augustinus
To 1 in. (3 cm)
Underwings are chocolate-brown.

Eastern Pine Elfin
Incisalia niphon
To 1.3 in. (3.5 cm)
Common in pine woodlands. Underwings are strikingly banded.

Coral Hairstreak
Harkenclenus titus
To 1.5 in. (4 cm)
Note reddish spots along margin of hindwings. Upperwings are brownish.
Underwings

Gray Hairstreak
Strymon melinus
To 1.25 in. (3.2 cm)
Dark grayish butterfly has orange spots on hindwings. Underwings are blue-gray. The most widespread hairstreak in North America.
Underwings

GOSSAMER-WINGED BUTTERFLIES

This family of small bluish or coppery butterflies often has small, hair-like tails on its hindwings. Most rest with their wings folded and underwings exposed.

Striped Hairstreak
Satyrium liparops
To 1.25 in. (3.2 cm)
Underwings are marked by thin white stripes.
Underwings

Banded Hairstreak
Satyrium calanus
To 1.25 in. (3.2 cm)
Rests with wings folded and underwings exposed. Upperwings are brownish.
Underwings

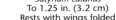

SKIPPER

Named for their fast, bouncing flight, skippers have distinctive antennae that end in curved clubs.

Silver-spotted Skipper
Epargyreus clarus
To 2.5 in. (6 cm)
Has a large, irregular silver patch on the underside of its hindwings. Patch is absent on the forewings.

Hobomok Skipper
Poanes hobomok
To 1.5 in. (4 cm)

European Skipper
Thymelicus lineola
To 1 in. (3 cm)
Note white fringes on wings.

Northern Cloudywing
Thorybes pylades
To 1.75 in. (4.5 cm)
Common in open areas.

Peck's Skipper
Polites peckius
To 1 in. (3 cm)
Underwings have large yellow patches.

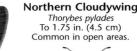

Dreamy Duskywing
Erynnis icelus
To 1.5 in. (4 cm)
Note silvery patches on outer forewings.

This family is named for its small forelegs that they use to "taste" food.

Milbert's Tortoiseshell
Aglais milberti
To 2 in. (5 cm)

Hackberry Emperor
Asterocampa celtis
To 2.5 in. (6 cm)
Is gray-brown to orange.

Viceroy
Limenitis archippus
To 3 in. (8 cm)
Told from similar Monarch by its smaller size and the thin, black band on its hindwings.

Little Wood Satyr
Megisto cymela
To 2 in. (5 cm)
Note 2 "eyespots" on each wing.

White Admiral
Limenitis arthemis
To 3 in. (8 cm)
Common in upland deciduous forests.

Common Ringlet
Coenonympha tullia
To 1.5 in. (4 cm)

Red-spotted Purple
Limenitis arthemis astyanax
To 3.5 in. (9 cm)

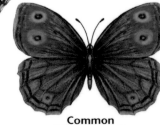

Common Wood Nymph
Cercyonis pegala
To 3 in. (8 cm)
Note 2 "eyespots" on the forewing. Yellow band is not always present.

American Snout
Libytheana carinenta
To 2 in. (5 cm)
"Snout" is formed from projecting mouth parts which enclose its coiled proboscis.

Northern Pearly-eye
Enodia anthedon
To 2 in. (5 cm)
Common in clearings and deciduous woodlands.

Monarch
Danaus plexippus
To 4 in. (10 cm)
Note rows of white spots on edges of wings.

Aphrodite Fritillary
Speyeria aphrodite
To 3 in. (8 cm)
Hindwings are silver-spotted.

Silver-bordered Fritillary
Boloria selene
To 2 in. (5 cm)
Underwings feature rows of metallic silver spots.

Great Spangled Fritillary
Speyeria cybele
To 3 in. (8 cm)
Common in marshes and wet meadows.

Common Buckeye
Junonia coenia
To 2.5 in. (6 cm)
Note orange wing bars on forewings and eight distinct "eyespots."

Mourning Cloak
Nymphalis antiopa
To 3.5 in. (9 cm)
Emerges during the first spring thaw.

Compton Tortoiseshell
Nymphalis vaualbum
To 3 in. (8 cm)
Note ragged wings.

Eastern Comma
Polygonia comma
To 2 in. (5 cm)
Has a silvery comma mark on the underside of its hindwings.

Pearl Crescent
Phyciodes tharos
To 1.5 in. (4 cm)
Note black margins on wings. Hindwing is marked with dark crescent-shaped spots.

Question Mark
Polygonia interrogationis
To 2.5 in. (6 cm)
Note lilac margin on wings. Silvery mark on underwings resembles a question mark or semicolon.

Baltimore Checkerspot
Euphydryas phaeton
To 2.5 in. (6 cm)

American Lady
Vanessa virginiensis
To 2 in. (5 cm)
Underside of hindwings feature prominent "eyespots."

Red Admiral
Vanessa atalanta
To 2.5 in. (6 cm)
Note orange bars on forewings and border of hindwings.

Painted Lady
Vanessa cardui To 2.5 in. (6 cm)
Tip of forewing is dark with white spots.

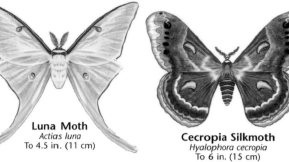

Luna Moth
Actias luna
To 4.5 in. (11 cm)

Cecropia Silkmoth
Hyalophora cecropia
To 6 in. (15 cm)
Note white, crescent-shaped marks on hindwings.

Fall Webworm Moth
Hyphantria cunea
To 1.5 in. (4 cm)
Larvae live in a communal web and feed on over 100 species of trees.

Hummingbird Clearwing
Hemaris thysbe
To 2 in. (5 cm)
Wings have clear patches. Hovers near flowers like a hummingbird.

Eight-Spotted Forester
Alypia octomaculata
To 1 in. (3 cm)
Forewing spots are yellowish. Active during the day.

Eastern Tent Caterpillar Moth
Malacosoma spp.
To 1.5 in. (4 cm)
Communal web nests are a common sight in fruit trees in spring.

Polyphemus Moth
Antheraea polyphemus
To 6 in. (15 cm)

Woolly Bear Caterpillar Moth
Pyrrharctia isabella
To 2 in. (5 cm)
Also called Isabella Tiger Moth. Caterpillar is distinctive.

About 75% of the crop plants grown worldwide depend on pollinators – bees, butterflies, birds, bats and other animals – for fertilization and reproduction. Although some species of plants are pollinated by the wind and water, the vast majority (almost 90%) need the help of animals to act as pollinating agents. More than 1,000 of the world's most important foods, beverages and medicines are derived from plants that require pollination by animals.

Pollinating animals worldwide are threatened due to loss of habitat, introduced and invasive species, pesticides, diseases and parasites.

Bees, Wasps & Flies

North America is home to approximately 4,000 species of bees. Of these, the most important crop pollinators are wild native honey bees and managed colonies of European honey bees. Other important flying insects include bumble bees, mason bees, carpenter bees, wasps and numerous flies. With honey bee populations in huge decline due to certain illnesses and habitat loss, this can have a huge impact on food production in North America.

HONEY BEE ANATOMY

Beetles

The living jewels of the bug world, beetles are the dominant life group on the earth with about 400,000 species found in all habitats except the polar regions and the oceans. They are invaluable to ecosystems as both pollinators and scavengers, feeding on dead animals and fallen trees to recycle nutrients back into the soil. Some, however, are serious pests and cause great harm to living plants (trees, crops). Learn to recognize the good from the bad and involve your local land management and pest control resources to mitigate the spread of harmful beetles.

BEETLE ANATOMY

Birds, Bats & Other Animals

More than 50 species of North American birds occasionally feed on plant nectar and blossoms, but it is the primary food source for hummingbirds and orioles. Sugar water feeders are a good way to supplement the energy of nectar drinkers, but it is far better to plant flowers and shrubs that provide native sources of nutrient-rich nectar. While very common in tropical climates around the world, only three species of nectar-feeding bats are found in the southwestern U.S. They are important pollinators of desert plants including large cacti (organ pipe, saguaro), agaves and century plants. Rodents, lizards and small mammals like mice also pollinate plants when feeding on their nectar and flower heads.

Ruby-throated Hummingbird

Long-nosed Bat

Attracting Bees & Other Pollinators

- Recognize the pollinators in your area and plant gardens to support the larvae and adults of different species.
- Cultivate native pollen and nectar-producing plants that bloom at different times throughout the growing season. Ensure the species you select will thrive with the amount of sunshine and moisture at the site. Reduce/eliminate use of pesticides. If you use any type of repellent, ensure it is organic and pesticide-free.
- The plants that attract birds, butterflies and moths for pollination most commonly have bright red, orange or yellow flowers with very little scent. Butterflies prefer flat-topped "cluster" flowers. Hummingbirds prefer tube or funnel-shaped flowers.
- Create areas, out of the sun, where pollinators can rest and avoid predation while foraging.
- Supply water for both drinking and bathing. Create shallow puddles for butterflies.
- Create nesting boxes or brushy areas that provide protection from predation and are suitable for pollinators to raise their young.
- Learn to recognize the good and bad garden bugs.

CATERPILLARS

Pipevine Swallowtail

Spicebush Swallowtail

Giant Swallowtail

Eastern Tailed Blue

Monarch

Mourning Cloak

Great Spangled Fritillary

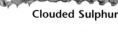
Silver-spotted Skipper

Woolly Bear Caterpillar Moth

Clouded Sulphur

Tent Caterpillar Moth

Fall Webworm Moth

Webworm Web

Tent Caterpillar Web